Contents

Paper from Fibres

Paper is made from fibrous natural materials like wood or cotton. The Chinese made paper from fibres of flax and grass. The ancient Egyptians used papyrus stems; the word 'paper' is derived from the word papyrus. In Bangladesh today, paper is made from waste jute and water hyacinths.

Most of our paper is made from wood. Wood is rigid because it contains lignin in its cell walls. Lignin causes white paper to turn yellow when exposed to sunlight. Old newspapers develop an extremely yellowed appearance.

Decorative figure of a woman holding a fish made in papier mâché by Julie Arkel.

Creating Art from Paper

Developing countries have led the world in the use of found materials for craftwork. At first, this was because of poverty and lack of resources but today there is a worldwide demand for such works of art. Often the original product names are still visible on the finished artefacts.

Papier mâché plate made at Srinigar, in the Indian province of Kashmir.

In Haiti, cement bags are recycled and turned into papier mâché from which beautiful decorated models are created. In Thailand, newspaper is recycled by craftspeople. Miniature baskets are made from newspaper strips wound round wire. Off-cuts of mulberry paper left over by kite makers are used to make boxes. Peruvian women make rolled paper necklaces out of coiled strips of paper cut from magazines – the strips are barely 1 mm wide.

ART FROM PAPER

with projects using waste paper and printed materials

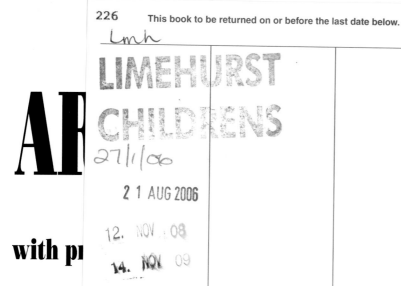

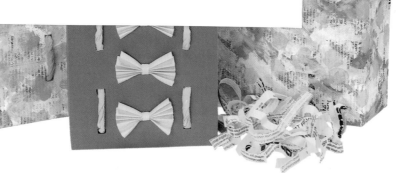

Gillian Chapman & Pam Robson

Art from Fabric
Art from Packaging
Art from Paper
Art from Rocks and Shells
Art from Sand and Earth
Art from Wood

For more information on this series and other Hodder Wayland titles go to www.hodderwayland.co.uk

This book was prepared for Wayland (Publishers) Ltd
by Globe Education, Nantwich, Cheshire
Artwork and design by Gillian Chapman
Photography by Rupert Horrox

First published in 1995 by Wayland (Publishers) Ltd

This paperback edition published in 2005 by Hodder Wayland, an imprint of Hodder Children's Books

Printed in China

British Library Cataloguing in Publication Data
Chapman, Gillian
Art from Paper. –(Salvaged series)
I. Title. II. Robson, Pam. III. Series
745.54

ISBN 0 7502 4783 5

Hodder Children's Books
A division of Hodder Headline Limited
338 Euston Road, London NW1 3BH

Trees

Re-using paper and cards helps to save our forests and woodlands whilst also conserving energy. Most paper is made from softwood trees, like spruce, which grow faster than hardwoods. However, fast-growing softwood plantations are unsuitable as habitats for vital ecosystems. Many plants and animals rely upon mixed woodland and forests for their survival.

Recycled Paper

Today, many everyday paper products are made from recycled paper. This book suggests useful ways to re-use paper and card. We should recycle paper products, not only to save our trees but also to reduce the mountains of waste accumulating on the Earth. Many towns now have collection points for recyclable items like paper, aluminium cans and glass.

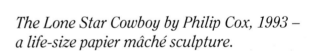

The Lone Star Cowboy by Philip Cox, 1993 – a life-size papier mâché sculpture.

Newspaper packed up ready for recycling in Andorra.

Always sort rubbish, only throwing away those things that cannot be recycled. A lot of the waste that is thrown into rubbish bins is deposited in landfill sites where dangerous gases can build up. Sometimes these gases are used to produce energy. Waste is also disposed by incineration or burning – but this causes toxic fumes to collect in the atmosphere. We live in a fast-moving, disposable society. The Earth's natural resources are limited. If we make best use of our rubbish those resources will last much longer.

Patterns in Paper

Collecting Waste Papers

Many people think of waste paper as rubbish, but it has many uses. It also has some amazing qualities. Paper can be rough, tough, delicate, smooth, translucent, opaque, light or heavy. Waste printed papers can be colourful, interesting and are mostly free.

Start to make a paper collection now and see how many types of paper you can find. Collect labels, tickets, cards, paper wrappers, envelopes, old sheets of music and maps, magazines and newspapers, junk mail, giftwrap, catalogues and brochures. Look for a range of colours and thicknesses. Not all scrap paper will be suitable for project work.

Sorting and Storing Paper

Each of the projects in this book requires a different kind of paper. Plain papers can be sorted according to their properties. Strong brown paper will need to be separated from delicate tissue paper. Printed papers can be sorted into colours, patterns, pictures or words. Organize your paper into different categories. Gummed or waxed paper cannot be recycled, so re-use envelopes if possible.

Keep paper away from direct sunlight, especially newspaper. Large pieces of paper are best stored flat. Smaller items, like old postcards, tickets and greetings cards can be kept in boxes.

Collection of Different Scrap Papers

Tearing Paper

Paper can be torn, cut and twisted into many forms. Its properties can be altered by folding and rolling. You can change the look and feel of the paper and make it stronger.

All paper is much easier to tear along the grain. To test for the grain direction, first tear across the sheet and then from top to bottom and notice the difference. Tearing paper along the edge of a ruler gives a neater finish.

Folding and Rolling

Thin paper will fold neatly, but thicker paper or card will need to be scored first with a blunt knife. Practise folding pieces of paper of different thicknesses making the folds as sharp as possible.

Make paper curls to decorate your models by wrapping long strips of paper tightly around a pencil. It is easier to roll paper into a tube or cylinder by rolling with the grain, this will make a tighter tube.

Pleating and Cutting

Make a series of small folds or pleats in a strip of paper. Fans of pleated papers can be used to decorate models.

Cutting simple patterns into paper with a craft knife can produce interesting textures but only do this when you have an adult to help.

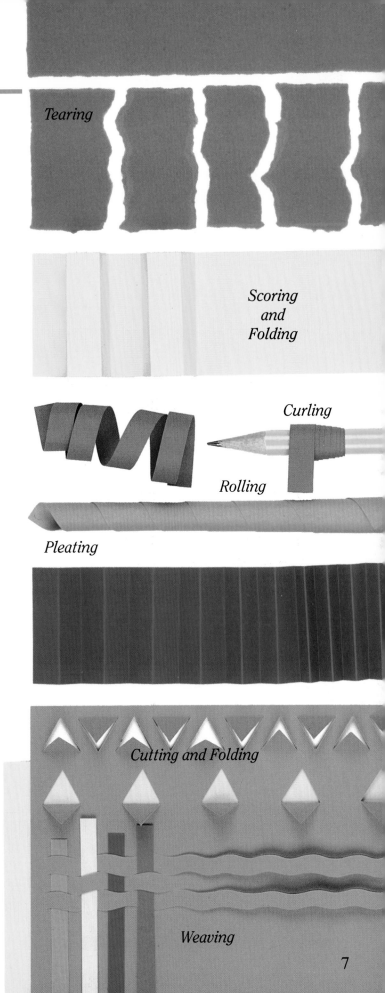

Tearing

Scoring and Folding

Curling

Rolling

Pleating

Cutting and Folding

Weaving

7

Paper Collage

Artists at Work

Many artists use found materials in their work. Both Matisse and Schwitters used different forms of scrap paper and printed material in their collages. The British artist, Philip Cox, began using cardboard and waste paper to make his life size figures because he could not afford to buy art materials.

Envelope Collages

Envelopes are ideal materials to use for an environmentally-friendly collage. They cannot be recycled because of the gum. Collect together envelopes of different shapes and colours to make your collage. Show the address side and the stamps if they are interesting, or have the flap open and tuck papers and messages inside.

Envelope Collage

Lettering Collage

Lettering

In newspapers and magazines, we see lettering in a range of styles and sizes. Create a monochrome collage by using different examples of lettering. Cut or tear single letters or blocks of newsprint into shapes contrasting light and dark tones.

Glueing Paper

Most water-based glues are ideal for paper but some thin papers will crinkle and distort if the glue is too wet. Test the glue first on scrap paper to make sure it is suitable. For very fine paper and tissue use a glue stick.

Paper Mosaic Collage

Patterns and Colours

An assortment of patterns and colours cut from printed paper makes an interesting mosaic picture. Work out your mosaic design first on a suitable background. Cut the coloured papers into small tile shapes. Arrange them according to your design, before sticking them down firmly.

Illustrations

Make a collection of pictures from magazines and brochures that relate to a particular theme, such as circular shapes. Mount them as a collage choosing a background material that complements the picture. Raise some of the images on card supports to give a 3-D effect.

Collage of Round Images

Collage in the Round

3-D Art from Paper

Picasso is well-known for his work both as a painter and a sculptor. He was the first major artist to use found objects in his artwork. Picasso's unique style of creating portraits can be seen in his 3-dimensional sculpted heads, especially those made from card and collage materials. The versatility of paper is noticeable when transforming flat sheets into a series of coiled shapes. Because paper is a flexible, fibrous material, it can be cut, coiled or folded into a variety of 3-dimensional shapes.

Coiling Paper

To make a coiled paper sculpture you will need to find, or make, a shallow box to contain the paper coils. Then make pattern divisions in the box from strips of card and glue them into place. Coil strips of paper of different colours and thicknesses. Position the coils in the box creating a pattern with them. By coiling strips of differing widths you can also create a 3-dimensional effect.

Coil strips of paper to make paper towers.

Wide strips make tall coils.   *Narrow strips make small coils.*

Coiled Paper Collage (from above)

Place the coils inside a box to make a pattern.

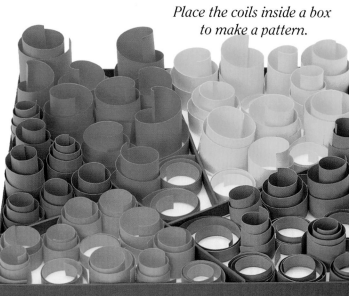

Coiled Paper Collage (from the side)

Sketches of the Head

Paper Sculptures

When making a 3-dimensional paper sculpture you must first select suitably rigid paper or card. The separate pieces will be slotted together and the finished sculpture must be strong enough to support itself. You can glue several sheets of paper together to achieve the necessary rigidity.

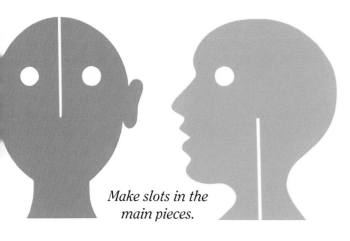

Make slots in the main pieces.

Paper Portraits

To make a 3-D portrait you must first make sketches of a head both in profile and full-face. Sketch someone you know or make an imaginary portrait. Consider all aspects of the head – the face and features, plus the back of the head and neck. It may help you to look at some of Picasso's work. Keep the shapes simple.

Find suitable card and work on the individual pieces separately. Cut out the shapes – the profiles, features and slots – before adding any details. Finally slot the pieces together when they are complete.

Paper Portraits

Picture Boxes

Collecting Printed Items

By now you will have probably gathered together lots of small printed items amongst your waste paper collection. Material such as labels, greetings cards, stamps and stickers can be very colourful and interesting. Sort them according to colour, pattern or theme.

Collection of Printed Printed Items

Decoupage

Decoupage is the art of decorating surfaces with paper cut-outs. You can use your collection of small printed scraps to give a discarded box or container a brand new lease of life.

Start with something simple to cover, like an old cardboard folder or wallet. Choose a selection of scraps that will cover the surfaces. Arrange them, moving them around until you are pleased with the effect, and then glue them into place. PVA glue is ideal for sticking paper scraps to card but use it very sparingly.

Decorating the Folder

Fasten the folder by tying thread around card circles secured with split-pins.

paper tassel

Decorated Boxes

Old boxes can be transformed into useful storage containers and gift boxes by covering them with an assortment of attractive papers and scraps. Choose a sheet of used giftwrap or even an outdated road map. Do not forget to decorate the inside of your container with printed paper. Protect the decorated surfaces with a coat of diluted PVA glue.

Finishing Touches

If you are giving a decorated box to someone as a gift, cover it in materials which interest that person, for example stamps, postcards or sporting pictures. Make matching handles, hinges and fasteners for your box as shown here.

*Decorated Boxes
(above and below)*

Thread string through the box lid to make hinges.

Fold a strip of card to make a handle. Attach to the lid with split pins.

Jewellery Box

Travel Box

Paper Bags

Carriers

Nowadays millions of plastic carrier bags are used daily to carry shopping. Plastic may be strong, but to dispose of plastic items is a major problem for a world with too much rubbish. A single sheet of paper may tear easily, but layers of paper, glued together, can make a carrier bag as strong as a plastic bag.

Plan for Bag

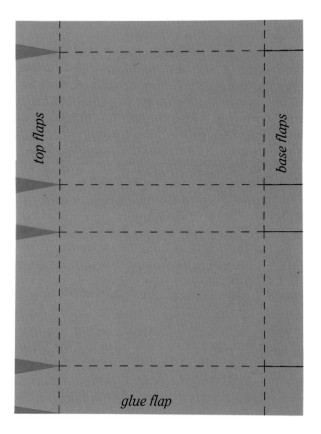

top flaps

base flaps

glue flap

Designing a Bag

The design for a bag must take into account a number of important considerations. The bag must be strong enough to take the weight of the contents. It also needs a strong but comfortable handle to make it user-friendly. Follow the diagram below choosing appropriate dimensions. Remember a very deep bag may drag on the floor. Finally, the bag should look attractive. If you decide to make it out of layers of newspaper, paint the paper first.

Assembling the Bag

Fold over top flaps.

Glue base flaps together.

Twisted Paper Handles

Extra Base

Folding and Glueing

Draw a plan first on to a large sheet of scrap paper. Cut out the shape and crease along the fold lines. It may help to score the fold lines first if the paper is thick. Try to make the creases as sharp as possible. Assemble the bag, glueing down the flaps as shown. Place an extra card base in the bag to reinforce the bottom.

Making the Handle

You can make a strong handle for the bag by twisting and glueing a long strip of newspaper into twine. Paint the handle to match the bag. Thread it through holes in the front and back of the bag. Pass it underneath for extra strength.

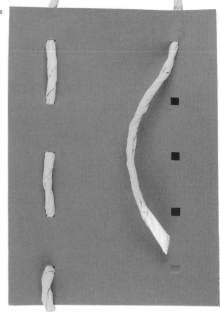

Threading the Handle

Gift Bags

You can also use discarded sheets of giftwrap or wallpaper. Decorate the bags with paint and coloured paper scraps. Shredded newspaper is an ideal packing material to protect fragile presents.

Gift Bag Ideas

Use shredded paper for packing.

Recycled Cards

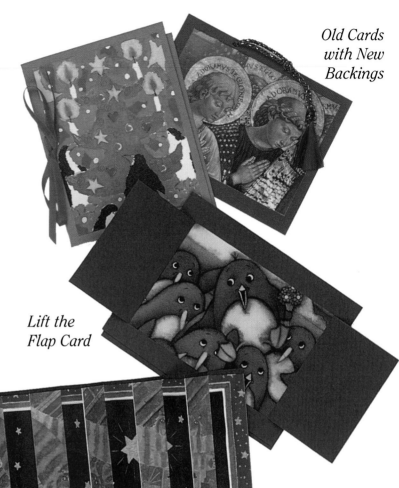

Old Cards with New Backings

Lift the Flap Card

Zigzag Card

Collage Cards

Recycling Cards

Sending greetings cards is traditional in many countries throughout the world. Cards are designed to suit every occasion. Some are printed on recycled paper, although many cards are not. Hundreds of thousands of trees are felled every year to make paper to print cards. In developed countries, these come from managed forests and the industry is big business. You can help in a small way to reduce the amount of new paper that is produced by making new cards out of old cards.

New Cards from Old

Many cards are too attractive to throw away. Here are some ideas for re-using them. Cut out pictures from old cards and glue them to new backing cards. Make a lift-the-flap card by cutting flaps in a folded card and glueing pictures behind. Cut two pictures into strips and glue them, alternately on to a pleated card to make a zigzag card. Make collage cards by glueing several pictures on to a folded card backing.

Pop-Up Cards

Find a picture to use as a backing for a pop-up. Fold the backing picture in half and measure a strip of card half the width of the card. Attach the strip to the backing, as shown here. Glue a folded pop-up picture to the strip. You have a new pop-up card.

A Card Holder

Some cards are really too special to recycle because they are hand-made or given by close family or friends. Here is an idea for making a card holder in which to keep them. Cut out the card holder shape from an old cereal packet, as shown. Cover the box with a patchwork of cards, glueing them down firmly. Thread string through a small hole in the top of the holder to hang it up.

Glue ends of strip to background and glue the pop-up to the strip.

Pop-Up Cards

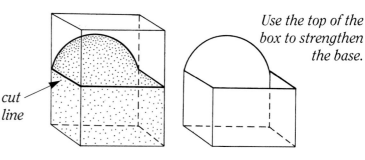

Use the top of the box to strengthen the base.

cut line

Making the Card Holder

Patchwork Card Holder

Gift Cards and Tags

Masks and Disguises

Disguises

African peoples traditionally carved masks out of wood to represent protective spirits. They were worn during religious ceremonies. The ancient Greeks used masks in the theatre to represent tragedy or comedy.

All masks are a form of disguise. A disguise may be required for a fancy dress masquerade. For this a half mask might be appropriate. It may be worn during a celebration such as Hallowe'en, where the aim is to frighten. For this a whole face mask would be more suitable.

Paper Disguises

All the paper disguises shown here are simple to make and fun to wear. Look through magazines for life-size photos of mouths, ears and eyes. Cut out as many examples as you can find. Include items of clothing, like hats; and also include jewellery and sunglasses.

All the cut-outs should be glued on to a backing card to strengthen them. Either keep single features separate, or make a large face by glueing several together. Finally attach each paper disguise to a stick to hold in front of your face.

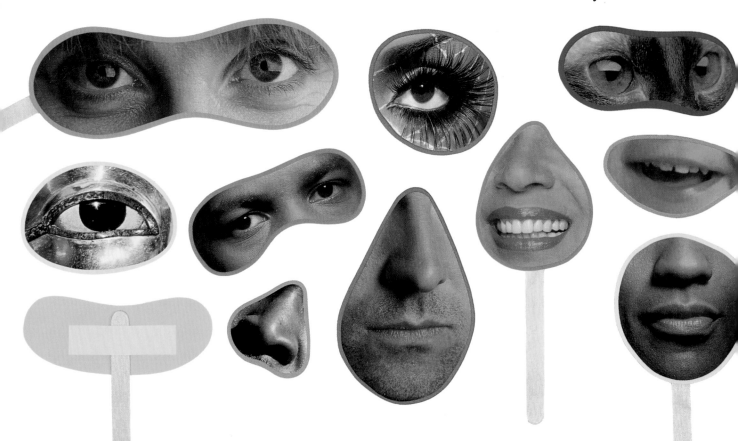

Paper Disguises – Half Masks

3-D Masks

These large paper masks are made to cover the whole head. They are made from a cylinder of paper that sits on the shoulders. First you will need to make a paper cylinder that fits over your head comfortably.

Tape or clip the cylinder together temporarily and ask a friend to mark the eye and mouth holes with a pencil. Undo the cylinder and cut out the holes with a craft knife. Roll the mask back into shape and hold it together with strong tape.

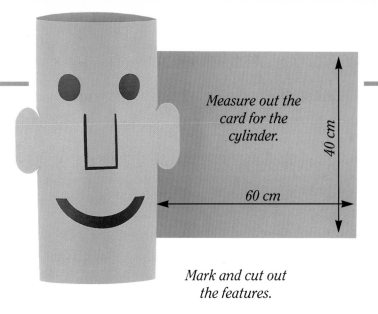

Measure out the card for the cylinder.

40 cm

60 cm

Mark and cut out the features.

Basic 3-D Mask

Decorating the Mask

You can add features, such as hair, plumes or feathers to the mask by cutting and folding them from scrap paper. Paint the mask with poster paints. Alternatively, use magazine cut-outs for the features.

Examples of Finished Masks

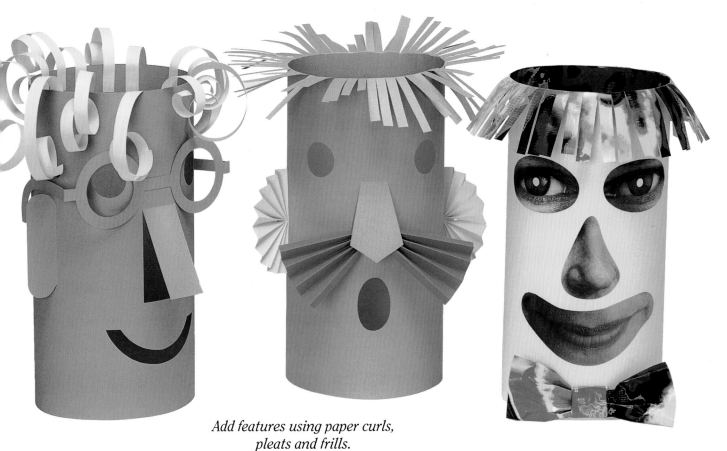

Add features using paper curls, pleats and frills.

19

Stuffed Shapes

Making Paper

Paper is made from the timber of spruces and firs which are the fastest growing conifers. Much water is needed to turn timber into wood pulp, so pulp mills are usually beside rivers. River pollution can result from the dirty water leaving a pulp mill and also from the chemical, dioxin, made during the bleaching of paper.

Stuffing Shapes

Clean waste paper can be saved and used. It is ideal as a stuffing material because it can be crumpled into balls. Sheets of newspaper, glued together make a strong fabric to hold the stuffing.

A Paper Mountain

At the beginning of the twentieth century, schoolchildren wrote on slates. Exercise books did not exist. People used cotton handkerchiefs, not paper tissues. Today, disposable paper products create a mountain of paper rubbish. In the developed countries, each person uses about 120 kg of paper a year.

The waste paper in Britain in one year is equal to 130 million trees. Recycling saves trees. Items like egg boxes are now made from recycled paper.

Making The Basic Shape To Be Stuffed

Leave opening for stuffing.

Tear paper into small squares.

Attach together by glueing, stapling or sewing.

Stuffed Animals

Decide on an animal to shape and make your basic shape from newspaper, stuffed with crumpled paper balls. The fish has fins and a tail made from pleated newspaper stapled or glued into place. The horse has a stuffed paper bag head, with a curled paper mane. The stick is rolled newspaper. For instructions on pleating, curling and rolling paper see page 7.

Making the Fish

Staple or glue the opening attaching the tail at the same time.

Hobby Horse

paper curls

paper ears

Place the stick across the top of the stuffed head and tape into place.

Finished Fish

Paint the stuffed animals with poster paints.

21

Bangles, Beads, Bowls

Papier Mâché

Paper combined with liquid paste produces a strong material called papier mâché. The liquid paste fills the holes in the surface of the paper to form a bond that sets hard.

Articles made from papier mâché date back to the invention of paper in the second century AD. The Chinese used papier mâché to make masks for their warriors, as it was both lightweight and strong. In the seventeenth century, decorative papier mâché boxes and toys were hardened with lacquer.

Papier mâché items were imported into Europe from eastern Asia. As a result of its popularity and versatility, factories in Russia, Europe and America, produced a fantastic range of papier mâché, from small snuff boxes to furniture. It has also been used to build a boat, a Norwegian church and a complete village in Australia.

There are two ways of making papier mâché – by 'layering' paper strips and glue over a mould, and by 'pulping' paper. The second method is ideal for moulding small shapes, such as jewellery.

Forming beads over a knitting needle.

Making Paper Pulp Jewellery

Paint beads with poster paints and thread on to cord.

Forming the pulp over a card roll.

Painted Bangles

Paper Pulp Jewellery

To make paper pulp, fill a large bowl with small pieces of torn newspaper. Cover the paper with warm water and leave to soak overnight. Strain off the water and add PVA glue, mashing the pulp until it feels like soft clay. Mould the pulp over a greased knitting needle to make beads. The bangles are shaped over empty sticky tape rolls.

Papier Mâché Bowls

You can make papier mâché bowls and plates by using plastic bowls and plates as moulds. First smear the plastic mould with a thin coat of cooking oil, then cover with cling film.

Start building up paper layers, glueing with diluted PVA glue. You can use strips of newspaper, but experiment with other coloured scrap paper. Try using torn pieces of tissue and crêpe paper, gift wrap and paper napkins.

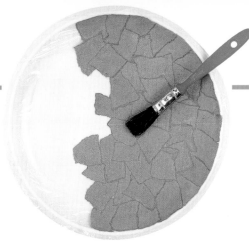

*Adding
Layers
of Paper*

Building Layers

You will need to build up at least six layers of papier mâché to make a firm shape and more if you are using a fine paper like tissue. It helps to use a different coloured paper to distinguish each layer. Leave to dry for several days before removing the mould. Either trim the rim and bind it with paper strips to make a neat edge, or leave it uneven. Bowls made from coloured scrap papers will not need painting.

*Papier Mâché
Plate and Bowl*

Handmade Paper

Recycling Paper

Recycling weakens and shortens the cellulose fibres in paper. Consequently, there is a limit to the number of times that you can keep on recycling it to make more paper.

In France, scientists have discovered how to store paper indefinitely by turning it into small, dry pellets which are used to make building blocks. In India, stationery is handmade from recycled cotton rags. The paper is often decorated with pressed flowers and grasses and usually exported to other countries.

Waste Paper

There is a vast quantity of waste paper suitable for recycling. Newspapers are readily available but the pulp discolours because of the printing ink. For making handmade papers try to find a better quality paper, such as discarded computer or photocopier paper.

Basic Equipment

You will need a papermaking frame, like the one shown here. Ask an adult to help you make one. It consists of two wooden frames of equal size. The top frame, or deckle, rests on top of the bottom frame, or mould. The mould is covered with a fine mesh or net curtaining.

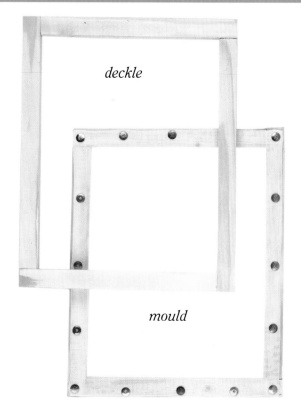

deckle

mould

Papermaking Frame

wood shavings

fresh and dried herbs

Materials for Papermaking

tea leaves and tea bags

How to Make Handmade Paper

Tear up the waste paper, cover with warm water and leave to soak overnight. Squeeze out handfuls of the soaked paper and put them into a bowl covering with fresh water. Mash to a smooth pulp using your hands or a potato masher. At this stage you can add any textured materials to the pulp.

Slide the mould into the pulp with the deckle on top. Shake it gently to spread the pulp evenly over the netting. Lift out and leave to drain. Remove the deckle and turn the mould over carefully on to an absorbent cloth. Press the netting with an old sponge to remove as much water as possible.

Lift the mould slowly, leaving your sheet of paper on the cloth. Lay another cloth on top of the paper and then put an old newspaper on top. Repeat the process until all the pulp has been used.

Cover the floor with thick newspaper and place the pile of cloths and newspaper in the middle. Put a board on top and gently stand on it to squeeze as much water from the paper as possible. Then remove the board and lay each separate cloth out to dry in a warm place. Peel the sheets of paper from each cloth while still damp and leave them flat to dry completely.

Coloured waste papers were used to make the coloured papers (1-3). The textured papers had the following added: (4) potato peelings; (5) chopped leaves; (6) wood chippings; (7) dried parsley; (8) spinach; (9) tea leaves.

Making Books

The First Books

The first books only became possible with the development of the art of papermaking. Before then, sheets of parchment, made from animal hide, were bound together to make codexes and even earlier, the ancient Egyptians used papyrus to make scrolls.

Making a Book

To make a book with sewn pages and a strong bound cover you need to follow three simple stages. First you will need to sew the pages of the book, then make the cover and finally attach the pages inside.

Making the Cover

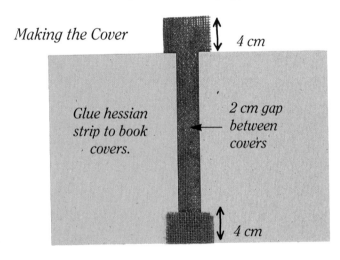

Glue hessian strip to book covers.

4 cm

2 cm gap between covers

4 cm

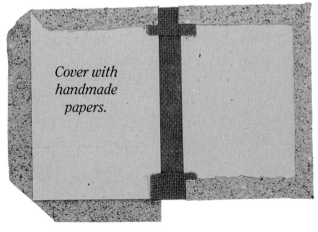

Cover with handmade papers.

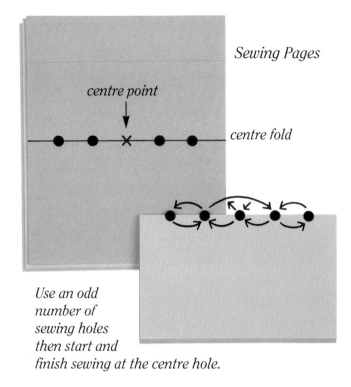

Sewing Pages

centre point

centre fold

Use an odd number of sewing holes then start and finish sewing at the centre hole.

Sewing Pages

Decide how many pages your book will need and cut paper to size. Lay the sheets together and fold neatly in half. Open up and secure with paper-clips before marking the centre point on the crease with a small cross. Mark evenly spaced sewing holes either side of the centre cross. Pierce the holes with a drawing pin before sewing the pages together, following the order shown in the diagram.

Making the Cover

Take two pieces of card, slightly larger than your page size and bind them together with hessian. Cut the hessian 10 cm wide and 8 cm longer than the cards and attach it as shown here. Cover the outside of the book with pieces of your handmade paper.

Attaching the Pages

To attach the sewn pages to the cover, glue the first page down inside the front cover and the last page inside the back cover. Take time over this and make sure the pages are straight.

Attaching Pages to Cover

Decorative Covers

We have used handmade papers to make the books shown here. The papers themselves are beautifully coloured and textured, and make ideal decorative book covers.

Books Made Using Handmade Papers and Textured Covers

Embossing Designs

It is also possible to create embossed patterns on the papers to make attractive covers. Damp the paper and impress coiled string, wire mesh or other raised images into the surface. Leave under a heavy weight until dry.

embossed design using chicken wire

embossed design using string

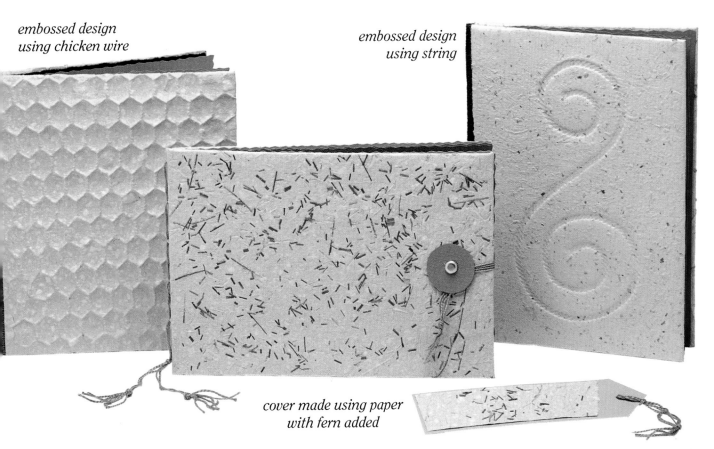

cover made using paper with fern added

Collecting Scraps

Scrap Books

By the end of the nineteenth century, many people in industrialized countries began to have more leisure time. Children were encouraged to spend their play time in useful ways. Collecting scraps became a popular leisure activity. Today the term 'scrap-book' has a much wider application. It can be used to display a collection of postcards, photographs, tickets, programmes, labels, stamps or other memorabilia.

Making a Scrap Book

Why not make a scrap book to hold your collection? Use recycled materials or your handmade papers to make the book. Follow the instructions on page 24 to sew pages together. Use scrap card for the covers and decorate them with appropriate items. There are many ways of mounting a collection. Some things can be stuck directly on to the pages. You could attach small transparent bags to your pages and slip items inside. They can then be repositioned if necessary.

Scrap-Books

Mix and Match Book

Cut out cartoon pictures from old greetings cards to make this amusing book. Follow the instructions on page 26. Cut across the pages, leaving a 1 cm space uncut either side of the centre fold. Now stick the cut out pictures on to the pages. Have fun making some strange people.

Storing Records

You can make a useful storage box in which to keep a photograph or postcard collection. Use the bottom of an old shoe box for the main drawer and make an outer cover from scrap card. Decorate the outside of the box. Make a series of blank record cards to slot in between the items in your collection so you can categorize them in order of subject or date.

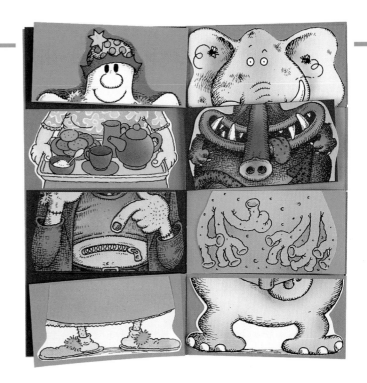

Mix and Match Book

Making the Record Box

glue

scrap card

shoe box

Box for Postcard Collection

Decorate the box with a postcard collage.

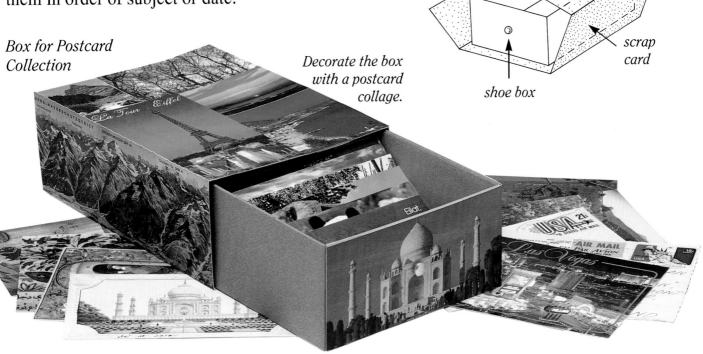

Glossary

codex (plural: codices) A volume of manuscripts of ancient text.

conifers Trees or shrubs bearing cones and evergreen leaves. The group includes pines, spruces, firs and larches.

decoupage The decoration of a surface with cut out shapes or illustrations.

developed countries Highly industrialized countries such as those in Europe and North America; also Japan and Australia.

developing countries Countries that rely on agriculture but are becoming more industrialized such as most African, Asian and South American countries.

dioxin Any of various chemical by products resulting from the manufacture of certain herbicides and bactericides.

ecosystem The interaction between a community and its non-living environment.

embossed A surface with a raised decoration in low relief.

flax A plant with blue flowers. The fibrous stems are used to make linen thread.

hardwood Close-grain wood from deciduous trees.

hessian A strong coarse fabric made from jute and used to make sacking.

jute A tropical plant.

lacquer A hard shiny coating or varnish often used to protect furniture.

landfill sites Low-lying tips filled up with layers of rubbish and earth.

lignin A part of the cell walls of certain plants, making the plant rigid.

memorabilia Important items from the past.

methane A gas which can be burned and used as fuel.

monochrome Black and white artwork.

opaque Refers to a material that does not transmit light.

papyrus Paper made by the ancient Egyptians from the stems of an aquatic plant.

parchment Durable manuscript material made from treated animal skin.

profile A side view of the head.

snuff box A small box for snuff (powdered tobacco).

softwood Open-grained wood from conifers.

toxic fumes Poisonous fumes.

translucent Semi-transparent, allowing the passage of a certain amount of light.

More Information

Fiarotta, Noel & Phyllis *Papercrafts Around the World*
(Sterling Juvenile Books, 2000)
Llewellyn, C. *Material World: Paper* (Franklin Watts, 2001)
Newcomb, R. & Rhatigan, J. *Paper Fantastic: 50
Creative Projects* (Lark Books, 2004)
Pickering Rothamel, Susan *The Art of Paper Collage*
(Sterling Publishing, 2001)
Robins, Deri *Making Papier Mâché*
(Kingfisher Books, 2001)
Walker, Kate *Recycle, Reduce, Reuse, Rethink: Paper*
(Smart Apple Media, 2004)
Watson, David *Creative Handmade Paper*
(Search Press Ltd, 1991)
Watson, David *Papermaking* (Search Press Ltd, 2000)

Australian Conservation Foundation, Floor 1,
60 Leicester Street, Carlton, Vic 3035

Confederation of Paper Industries, 1 Rivenhall Road,
Swindon, Wilshire, SN5 7BD

British Museum, Great Russell Street, London, WC1B 3DG
Museum of London, 150 London Wall, London, EC2Y 5HN
Science Museum, Exhibition Road, London, SW7 2DD

Traidcraft, Kingsway, Gateshead, Tyne & Wear NE11 0NE
Specialist Crafts Ltd, Unit 2B, Wanlip Road Industrial Estate,
Syston, Leicester, LE7 1PD

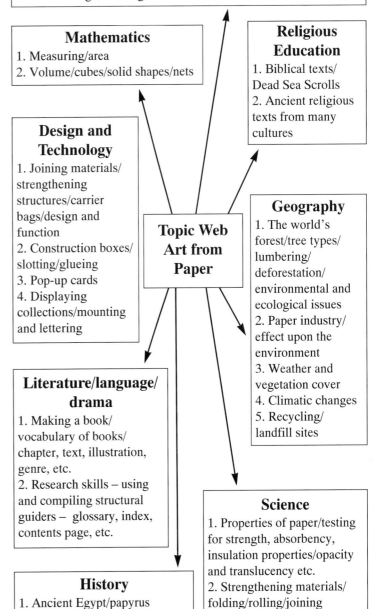

Art and Craft
1. Artists/Matisse/Picasso/Schwitters/Philip Cox
2. Collage/decoupage/papier mâché/sculpture/mask-making/
model-making/making paper
3. Texture/pattern/colour
4. Poster design/lettering/illuminated letters

Mathematics
1. Measuring/area
2. Volume/cubes/solid shapes/nets

Religious Education
1. Biblical texts/
Dead Sea Scrolls
2. Ancient religious
texts from many
cultures

Design and Technology
1. Joining materials/
strengthening
structures/carrier
bags/design and
function
2. Construction boxes/
slotting/glueing
3. Pop-up cards
4. Displaying
collections/mounting
and lettering

**Topic Web
Art from
Paper**

Geography
1. The world's
forest/tree types/
lumbering/
deforestation/
environmental and
ecological issues
2. Paper industry/
effect upon the
environment
3. Weather and
vegetation cover
4. Climatic changes
5. Recycling/
landfill sites

**Literature/language/
drama**
1. Making a book/
vocabulary of books/
chapter, text, illustration,
genre, etc.
2. Research skills – using
and compiling structural
guiders – glossary, index,
contents page, etc.

History
1. Ancient Egypt/papyrus
2. Aztecs/bark paper
3. Middle Ages/parchment
Development of printing
4. Manuscripts
5. Books
6. Newspapers

Science
1. Properties of paper/testing
for strength, absorbency,
insulation properties/opacity
and translucency etc.
2. Strengthening materials/
folding/rolling/joining
3. Structures/bridges/tunnels
4. Changing the properties of
materials/composites/
mixtures/papier mâché

Index